HISTORY'S GREATEST WARRIORS

Zulu Warriors

by Aaron Trejo

BELLWETHER MEDIA • MINNEAPOLIS, MN

TM

Are you ready to take it to the extreme?
Torque books thrust you into the action-packed world
of sports, vehicles, mystery, and adventure. These books
may include dirt, smoke, fire, and dangerous stunts.
Warning: read at your own risk.

Library of Congress Cataloging-in-Publication Data

Trejo, Aaron.
 Zulu warriors / by Aaron Trejo.
    p. cm. -- (Torque: history's greatest warriors)
 Summary: "Engaging images accompany information about Zulu warriors. The combination of
high-interest subject matter and light text is intended for students in grades 3 through 7"--Provided by
publisher.
 Includes bibliographical references and index.
 ISBN 978-1-60014-633-6 (hardcover : alk. paper)
 1. Zulu (African people)--Wars--Juvenile literature. 2. Zulu (African people)--History--Juvenile
literature. 3. Zulu War, 1879--Juvenile literature. 4. Zululand (South Africa)--History--To 1879--Juvenile
literature. 5. Great Britain--Colonies--Africa--Juvenile literature. I. Title.
 DT1768.Z95T74 2012
 968.04'5--dc22
                                        2011003047

This edition first published in 2012 by Bellwether Media, Inc.

Contents

Who Were Zulu Warriors?

Zulu warriors were fierce fighters in southern Africa in the 1700s and 1800s. Common people made up Zulu armies called *impis*. They did not have advanced weapons. However, their **tactics** and bravery helped them defeat highly trained armies.

Shaka Zulu

In the late 1700s, a man named Shaka Zulu rose to power. He changed the way *impis* were organized and used in battle. The Zulu fought other African tribes to expand their territory. Their kingdom became powerful in the early 1800s.

A F R I C A

Zulu Kingdom

Zulu warriors were deadly in battle. *Impis* were divided into groups called **regiments**. Each regiment had Zulu warriors of the same age. Shaka did this so that each warrior in a regiment could move at the same speed. Shaka made sure that his warriors were **disciplined** and brave. He would have any warriors who ran from battle killed.

9

Zulu Warrior Training

All Zulu men learned to fight from a young age. Boys practiced using spears and clubs. They often traveled with warriors. They carried food, weapons, and other supplies needed for battle. Young men could be called to war in their late teens. They served in an *impi* until they married.

Zulu Fact

During warfare between tribes, enemy survivors had a choice. They could become Zulu warriors or be killed!

Zulu Battle Tactic:
The Beast's Horns

This famous tactic of the Zulu warriors enabled them to surprise and overwhelm the enemy.

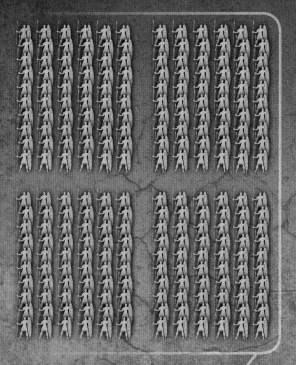

Loins

The loins included backup warriors who supported the chest and often finished off the enemy.

Chest

The chest included experienced warriors who moved from the middle to attack the enemy.

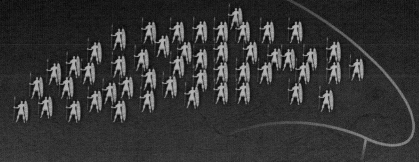

Left and Right Horns

The left and right horns included young, fast warriors who came from the left and right to surround and trap the enemy.

Enemy

Front Line

The front line included warriors who distracted the enemy and protected the chest from enemy fire.

Zulu Warrior Weapons and Gear

iklwa

Zulu warriors used spears and clubs. The *iklwa* was the main Zulu weapon. This spear had a short handle and a long blade. It was named for the sound it made when pulled out of a human body. The *ipapa* was a smaller spear. It could be thrown at enemies. The *knobkerrie* was a **blunt** weapon carved from a piece of wood. One end was shaped like a ball. It was perfect for breaking bones.

knobkerrie

Zulu Fact

Some Zulu warriors used guns they had taken from enemies on the battlefield.

Zulu Fact

Zulu warriors fought barefoot.
This allowed them to move quickly.
British soldiers often put broken glass
on the ground to slow them down.

Zulu warriors relied on their speed
in battle. They did not wear armor or
boots. Many wore animal skins or furs.
Some wore **headdresses** with fur or
feathers. Zulu warriors carried leather
shields. All shields belonged to the Zulu
king. The warriors returned their shields
to the king when a battle was over.

The Decline of Zulu Warriors

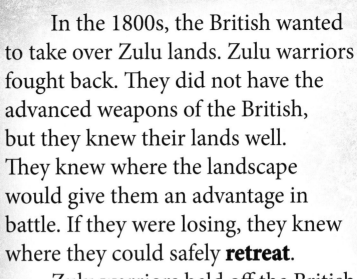

In the 1800s, the British wanted to take over Zulu lands. Zulu warriors fought back. They did not have the advanced weapons of the British, but they knew their lands well. They knew where the landscape would give them an advantage in battle. If they were losing, they knew where they could safely **retreat**.

Zulu warriors held off the British for a few years. However, the British began using new, powerful guns. The **Gatling gun** could shoot 200 rounds per minute. The Zulu had no defense against this kind of firepower.

Gatling gun

Zulu Fact

To many South Africans, January 22 is known as the Day of the Zulu. On that day in 1879, an *impi* defeated the British at the Battle of Isandlwana.

The Battle of Kambula took place in 1879. Around 20,000 Zulu warriors fought against 2,000 British soldiers. The British guns overpowered the Zulu. Around 3,000 Zulu warriors died.

The loss of this battle broke the spirit of the Zulu warriors. They could no longer defend their lands from the British. The time had come for the great Zulu warriors to put down their weapons.

Glossary

blunt—not sharp

disciplined—showing order and control; Zulu warriors followed orders very well.

Gatling gun—a large gun that fires rounds very quickly

headdresses—decorative coverings worn on the head

regiments—groups of soldiers who fight together in land battles; Zulu regiments were organized by age group.

retreat—to fall back to a safer location

tactics—military strategies

To Learn More

AT THE LIBRARY

Dougherty, Terri. *Zulu Warriors*. Mankato, Minn.: Capstone Press, 2008.

Richardson, Hazel. *Life in Ancient Africa*. New York, N.Y.: Crabtree Pub. Co., 2005.

Stanley, Diane, and Peter Vennema. *Shaka: King of the Zulus*. New York, N.Y.: Mulberry Books, 1994.

ON THE WEB

Learning more about Zulu warriors is as easy as 1, 2, 3.

1. Go to www.factsurfer.com.

2. Enter "Zulu warriors" into the search box.

3. Click the "Surf" button and you will see a list of related Web sites.

With factsurfer.com, finding more information is just a click away.

Index